BRITISH POETS SERIES

William Shakespeare: *Selected Sonnets and Verse*
edited, with an introduction by Mark Tuley

Edmund Spenser: *Poems*
selected and introduced by Teresa Page

Robert Herrick: *Selected Poems*
edited and introduced by M.K. Pace

John Donne: *Poems*
selected and introduced by A.H. Ninham

Percy Bysshe Shelley: *Poems*
selected and introduced by Charlotte Greene

Sir Thomas Wyatt: *Love For Love: Selected Poems*
edited by Louise Cooper

Thomas Hardy: *Selected Poems*
edited, with an introduction by A.H. Ninham

Emily Bronte: *Poems*
selected and introduced by Teresa Page

John Keats: *Selected Poems*
edited with an introduction by Miriam Chalk

Henry Vaughan: *Poems*
selected and introduced by A.H. Ninham

The Crescent Moon Book of Love Poetry
edited by Louise Cooper

The Crescent Moon Book of Mystical Poetry in English
edited by Carol Appleby

The Crescent Moon Book of Nature Poetry From Langland to Lawrence
edited by Margaret Elvy

The Crescent Moon Book of Metaphysical Poetry
edited and introduced by Charlotte Greene

The Crescent Moon Book of Elizabethan Love Poetry
edited and introduced by Carol Appleby

The Crescent Moon Book of Romantic Poetry
edited and introduced by L.M. Poole

Blinded By Her Light The Love-Poetry of Robert Graves
by Jeremy Robinson

The Best of Peter Redgrove's Poetry: The Book of Wonders
by Peter Redgrove, edited and introduced by Jeremy Robinson

Peter Redgrove: Here Comes the Flood
by Jeremy Robinson

Sex-Magic-Poetry-Cornwall: A Flood of Poems
by Peter Redgrove, edited with an essay by Jeremy Robinson

Brigitte's Blue Heart
by Jeremy Reed

Claudia Schiffer's Red Shoes
by Jeremy Reed

By-Blows: Uncollected Poems
by D.J. Enright

*Shakespeare: Love, Poetry and Magic
in Shakespeare's Sonnets and Plays*
by B.D. Barnacle

Being Alive

Selected Poems

Being Alive

Selected Poems

D.H. LAWRENCE

Edited by Margaret Elvy

CRESCENT MOON

CRESCENT MOON PUBLISHING
P.O. Box 393
Maidstone
Kent, ME14 5XU
United Kingdom

First published 1994. Second edition 2008
Introduction © Margaret Elvy, 1994, 2008.

Printed and bound in Great Britain.
Set in Garamond Book 12 on 15pt.
Designed by Radiance Graphics.

The right of Margaret Elvy to be identified as the editor of *Being Alive: Selected Poems* has been asserted generally in accordance with sections 77 and 78 of the Copyright, Designs and Patents Act 1988.

British Library Cataloguing in Publication data

Lawrence, D.H.
Being Alive: Selected Poems. – (British Poets Series)
I. Title II. Elvy, Margaret
III. Series
821.912

ISBN 1-86171-144-1
ISBN-13 9781861711441

CONTENTS

Moonrise   11

Gloire de Dijon   12

Tropic   13

from Sicilian Cyclamens   14

from Fish   15

Leda   16

Swan   17

Loneliness   19

Future Religion   20

Trees in the Garden   21

Whales Weep Not!   22

Lucifer 25

Bavarian Gentians   26

from Resurrection   28

Moon New–Risen   30

Lightning   31

Touch Comes   33

Glory   34

Desire is Dead   35

When the Ripe Fruit Falls   36

Sun in Me   37

Being Alive   38

Space   39

Peacock   40

Fire   41

New Moon   42

Desire Goes Down Into the Sea   43

Conscience   44

Aware   45

Obscenity   46

Touch   47

Baby Tortoise   48

Tortoise Shout   52

Letter From Town   57

Afternoon In School   59

The White Horse   61

Pinao   62

Rose of All the World   63

New Year's Eve   65

from Craving For Spring   66

from Manifesto   68

A Note On D.H. Lawrence   75

MOONRISE

And who has seen the moon, who has not seen
Her rise from out the chamber of the deep,
Flushed and grand and naked, as from the chamber
Of finished bridegroom, seen her rise and throw
Confession of delight upon the wave,
Littering the waves with her own superscription
Of bliss, till all her lambent beauty shakes towards us
Spread out and known at last, and we are sure
That beauty is a thing beyond the grave,
That perfect, bright experience never falls
To nothingness, and time will dim the moon
Sooner than our full consummation here
In this odd life will tarnish or pass away.

GLOIRE DE DIJON

When she rises in the morning
I linger to watch her;
She spreads the bath-cloth underneath the window
And the sunbeams catch her
Glistening white on the shoulders,
While down her sides the mellow
Golden shadow glows as
She stoops to the sponge, and her swung breasts
Sway like full-blown yellow
Gloire de Dijon roses.

She drips herself with water, and her shoulders
Glisten as silver, they crumple up
Like wet and falling roses, and I listen
For the sluicing of their rain-dishevelled petals.
In the window full of sunlight
Concentrates her golden shadow
Fold on fold, until it glows as
Mellow as the glory roses.

TROPIC

Sun, dark sun,
Sun of black void heat,
Sun of the torrid mid–day's horrific darkness:

Behold my hair twisting and going black.
Behold my eyes turn tawny yellow
Negroid;
See the milk of northern spume
Coagulating and going black in my veins
Aromatic as frankincense.

Columns dark and soft,
Sunblack men,
Soft shafts, sunbreathing mouths,
Eyes of yellow, golden sand
As frictional, as perilous, explosive as brimstone.

Rock, waves of dark heat;
Waves of dark heat, rock, sway upwards.
Waver perpendicular.

What is the horizontal rolling of water
Compared to the flood of black heat that rolls upwards
                                        past my eyes?

from SICILIAN CYCLAMENS

Ah Mediterranean mornings, when our world began!
Far-off Mediterranean mornings,
Pelasgic faces uncovered,
And unbudding cyclamens.

The hare suddenly goes uphill
Laying back her long ears with unwinking bliss.

And up the pallid, sea-blenched Mediterranean
stone-slopes
Rose cyclamen, ecstatic fore-runner!
Cyclamens, ruddy-muzzled cyclamens
In little bunches like bunches of wild hares
Muzzles together, ears-aprick,
Whispering witchcraft
Like women at a well, the dawn-fountain.

from FISH

You and the naked element,
Sway-wave.
Curvetting bits of tin in the evening light.

Who is it ejects his sperm to the naked flood?
in the wave-mother?
Who swims enwombed?
Who lies with the waters of his silent passion, womb-
                                        element?
– Fish in the waters under the earth

LEDA

Come not with kisses
not with caresses
of hands and lips and murmurings;
come with a hiss of wings
and sea-touch tip of a beak
and treading of wet-webbed, wave-working feet
into the marsh-soft belly.

SWAN

Far-off
at the core of space
at the quick
of time
beats
and goes still
the great swan upon the waters of all endings
the swan within vast chaos, within the electron.

For us
no longer he swims calmly
nor clacks across the forces furrowing a great gay trail
of happy energy,
nor is he nestling passive upon the atoms,
nor flying north desolative icewards
to the sleep of ice,
nor feeding in the marshes,
nor honking horn-like into the twilight.

But he stoops, now
in the dark
upon us;
he is treading our women
and we men are put-out
as the vast white bird
furrows our featherless women
with unknown shocks

and stamps his black marsh-feet on their white and
marshy flesh.

LONELINESS

I never know what people mean when they complain of
                                            loneliness,
To be alone is one of life's greatest delights, thinking
                                one's own thoughts,
doing one's own little jobs, seeing the world beyond
and feeling oneself uninterrupted in the rooted
                                connection
with the centre of all things.

FUTURE RELIGION

The future of religion lies in the mystery of touch.
The mind is touchless,so is the will, so is the spirit.
First comes the death, then the pure aloneness, which is
                                permanent
then the resurrection into touch.

TREES IN THE GARDEN

Ah in the thunder air
how still the trees are!

And the lime-tree, lovely and tall, every leaf silent
hardly looses even a last breath of perfume.

And the ghostly, creamy coloured little tree of leaves
white, ivory white among the rambling greens
how evanescent, variegated elder, she hesitates on the
                              green grass
as if, in another moment, she would disappear
with all her grace of foam!

And the larch that is only a column, it goes up too tall to
                              see:
and the balsam pines that are blue with the grey-blue
blueness of things from the sea,
and the young copper beech, its leaves red-rosy at the
                              ends
how still they are together, they stand so still
in the thunder air, all strangers to one another
as the great grass glows upwards, strangers in the silent
                              garden.

WHALES WEEP NOT!

They say the sea is cold, but the sea contains
the hottest blood of all, and the wildest, the most
                                        urgent.

All the whales in the wider deeps, hot are they, as they
                                        urge
on and on, and dive beneath the icebergs.
The right whales, the sperm-whales, the
                        hammer-heads, the killers
there they blow, there they blow, hot wild white breath
                        out of the sea!

And they rock, and they rock, through the sensual
                        ageless ages
on the depths of the seven seas,
and through the salt they reel with drunk delight
and in the tropics tremble they with love
and roll with massive, strong desire, like gods.
Then the great bull lies up against his bride
in the blue deep bed of the sea,
as mountain pressing on mountain, in the zest of life:
and out of the inward roaring of the inner red ocean of
                        whale-blood
the long tip reaches strong intense, like the
                        maelstrom-tip, and comes to rest
in the clasp and the soft, wild clutch of a she-whale's
                        fathomless body.

And over the bridge of the whale's strong phallus,
                    linking the wonder of whales
the burning archangels under the sea keep passing,
                    back and forth,
keep passing, archangels of bliss
from him to her, from her to him, great Cherubim
that wait on whales in mid-ocean, suspended in the
                    waves of the sea
great haven of whales in the waters, old hierarchies.

And enormous mother whales lie dreaming suckling
                    their whale-tender young
and dreaming with strange eyes wide open in the
                    waters of the beginning and the end.

And bull-whales gather their women and whale-calves
                    in a ring
when danger threatens, on the surface of the ceaseless
                    flood
and range themselves like great fierce Seraphims facing
                    the threat
encircling their huddled monsters of love.
And all this happens in the sea, in the salt
where God is also love, but without words:
and Aphrodite is the wife of whales
most happy, happy she!

and Venus among the fishes skips and is a she-dolphin
she is the gay, delighted porpoise sporting with love and
                    the sea
she is the female tunny-fish, round and happy among
                    the males

and dense with happy blood, dark rainbow bliss in the
sea.

LUCIFER

Angels are bright still, though the brightest fell.
But tell me, tell me, how do you know
he lost any of his brightness in the falling?
In the dark-blue depths, under layers and layers of
          darkness,
I see him more like the ruby, a gleam from within of his
          own magnificence,
coming like the ruby in the invisible dark, glowing
with his own annunciation, towards us.

BAVARIAN GENTIANS

Not every man has gentians in his house
in soft September, at slow, sad Michaelmas.

Bavarian gentians, big and dark,only dark
darkening the day-time, torch-like with the smoking
                              blueness of Pluto's gloom,
ribbed and torch-like, with their blaze of darkness
                              spread blue
down flattening into points, flattened under the sweep
                              of white day
torch-flower of the blue-smoking darkness, Pluto's
                              dark-blue daze,
black lamps from the halls of Dis, burning dark blue,
giving off darkness, blue darkness, as Demeter's pale
                              lamps give off light,
lead me, then, lead the way.

Reach me a gentian, give me a torch!
let me guide myself with the blue, forked torch of this
                              flower
down the darker and darker stairs, where blue is
                              darkened on blueness
even where Persephone goes, just now, from the
                              frosted September
to the sightless realm where darkness is awake upon
                              the dark
and Persephone herself is but a voice
or a darkness invisible enfolded in the deeper dark
of the arms Plutonic, and pierced with the passion of

dense gloom,
among the splendour of torches of darkness, shedding
darkness on the lost bride and her groom.

from RESURRECTION

Now, like a crocus in the autumn time,
My soul comes lambent from the endless night
Of death – a cyclamen, a crocus flower
Of windy autumn when the winds all sweep
The hosts away to death, where heap on heap
The dead are burning in the funeral wind.

•

Now like a cyclamen, a crocus flower
In autumn, like to a messenger come back
From embassy in death, I issue forth
Amid the autumn rushing red about
The bitter world, amid the smoke
From burning fires of many smouldering lives,
All bitter and corroding to the grave.

•

And still against the dark and violent wind,
Against the scarlet and against the red
And blood-brown flux of lives that sweep their way
In hosts towards the everlasting night,
I lift my little pure and lambent flame,
Unquenchable of wind or hosts of death
Or storms of tears, or rage, or blackening rain
Of full despair, I lift my tender flame
Of pure and lambent hostage from the dead –
Ambassador from halls of noiseless death.,

He who returns again from out the tomb
Dressed in the grace of immortality,
A fragile stranger in the flux of lives
That pour cascade-like down the blackening wind
Of sheer oblivion.

MOON NEW-RISEN

I saw the sky was lit
    Behind the sand-hills
But when I crossed the dunes
    And the moon stood opposite
      I was afraid.

For the golden moon communes
    With the darkness opposite
And small on the sand swills
    The sea, afraid
      To interrupt,
      But I, abrupt
Broke into the privacy
    Of the moon and the night:
The moon was in love, and she
Looked up at the night, and he
    Kissed her deliciously,
    And the world was alight.

LIGHTNING

I felt the lurch and halt of her heart
  Next my breast, where my own heart was
      beating;
And I laughed to feel it plunge and bound,
And strange in my blood-swept ears was the sound
  Of the words I kept repeating,
Repeating with tightened arms, and the hot blood's
      blindfold art.

Her breath flew warm against my neck,
  Warm as a flame in the close night air;
And the sense of her clinging flesh was sweet
Where her arms and my neck's blood-surge could
      meet.
  Holding her thus, did I care
That the black night hid her from me, blotted out every
      speck?

I leaned me forward to find her lips,
  And claim her utterly in a kiss,
When the lightning flew across her face,
And I saw her for the flaring space
  Of a second, afraid of the clips
Of my arms, inert with dread, wilted in fear of my kiss.

A moment, like a wavering spark,
  Her face lay there before my breast,
Pale lovelost in a snow of fear,

And guarded by a glittering tear,
      And lips apart with dumb cries;
A moment, and she was taken again in the merciful
                        dark.

I heard the thunder, and felt the rain,
      And my arms fell loose,a and I was dumb.
Almost I hated her, she was so good,
Hated myself, and the place, and my blood,
      Which burned with rage, as I bade her come
Home, away home, ere the lightning floated forth again.

TOUCH COMES

Touch comes when the white mind sleeps
and only then.
Touch comes slowly, if ever; it seeps
slowly up in the blood of men
and women.

Soft slow sympathy
of the blood in me, of the blood in thee
rises and flushes insidiously
over the conscious personality
of each of us, and covers us
with a soft one warmth, and a generous
kindled togetherness, so we go
into each other as tides flow
under a moon they do not know.

Personalities exist apart;
and personal intimacy has no heart.
Touch is of the blood
uncontaminated, the unmental flood.

When again in us
the soft blood softly flows together
towards touch, then this delirious
day of the mental welter and belter
will be passing away, we shall cease to fuss.

GLORY

Glory is of the sun, too, and the sun of suns,
and down the shafts of his splendid pinions
run tiny rivers of peace.

Most of his time, the tiger pads and slouches in a
                              burning peace.
And the small hawk high up turns round on the slow
                              pivot of peace.
Peace comes from behind the sun, with the peregrine
                              falcon, and the owl.
Yet all of these drink blood.

DESIRE IS DEAD

Desire may be dead
and still a man can be
a meeting place for sun and rain,
wonder outwaiting pain
as in a wintry tree.

WHEN THE RIPE FRUIT FALLS

When the ripe fruit falls
its sweetness distils and trickles away into
the veins of the earth.

When fulfilled people die
the essential oil of their experience enters
the veins of living space, and adds a glisten
to the atom,to the body of immortal chaos.

For space is alive
and it stirs like a swan
whose feathers glisten
silky with oil of distilled experience.

SUN IN ME

A sun will rise in me,
I shall slowly resurrect,
already the whiteness of false dawn is on my inner
                                        ocean.

A sun in me.
And a sun in heaven.
And beyond that, the immense sun behind the sun,
the sun of immense distances, that fold themselves
                                together
within the genitals of living space.
And further, the sun within the atom
which is god in the atom.

BEING ALIVE

The only reason for living is being fully alive;
and you can't be fully alive if you are crushed by secret
fear,
and bullied with the threat: get money, or eat dirt! –
and forced to do a thousand mean things meaner than
your nature,
and forced to clutch on to possessions in the hope
they'll make you feel safe,
and forced to watch everyone that comes near you, lest
they've come to do you down.

Without a bit of common trust in one another, we can't
live.
In the end, we go insane.
It is the penalty of fear and meanness, being meaner
than our natures are.

To be alive, you've got to feel a generous flow,
and under a competitive system that is impossible,
really.
The world is waiting for a new great movement of
generosity,
or for a great wave of death.
We must change the system, and make living free to all
men,
or we must see men die, and then die ourselves.

SPACE

Space, or course, is alive
that's why it moves about;
and that's what makes it eternally spacious and
                                        unstuffy.

And somewhere it has a wild heart
that sends pulses even through me;
and I call it the sun;
and I feel aristocratic, noble, when I feel a pulse go
                                through me
from the wild heart of space, that I call the sun of suns.

PEACOCK

Think how a peacock in a forest of high trees
shimmers in a stream of blueness and long-tressed
                                        magnificence!
And women even cut their shimmery hair!

FIRE

Fire is dearer to us than love or food,
hot, hurrying, yet it burns if you touch it.

What we ought to do
is not to add our love together, or our goodwill, or any
                                            of that,
for we're sure to bring in a lot of lies,
but our fire, our elemental fire
so that it rushes up in a huge blaze like a phallus into
                                            hollow space
and fecundates the zenith and the nadir
and sends off millions of sparks of new atoms
and singes us, and burns the house down.

NEW MOON

The new moon, of no importance
lingers behind as the yellow sun glares and is gone
beyond the sea's edge;
earth smokes blue;
the new moon, in cool height above the blushes,
brings a fresh fragrance of heaven to our senses.

DESIRE GOES DOWN INTO THE SEA

I have no desire any more
towards woman or man, bird, beast of creature or
                                      thing.

All day long I feel the tide rocking, rocking
though it strikes no shore
in me.

Only mid-ocean—.

CONSCIENCE

Conscience
is sun-awareness
and   our   deep   instinct
not to go against the sun.

AWARE

Slowly the moon is rising out of the ruddy haze,
Divesting herself of her golden shift, and so
Emerging white and exquisite; and I in amaze
See in the sky before me, a woman I did not know
I loved, but there she goes, and her beauty hurts my
                                                    heart;
I follow her down the night, begging her not to depart.

OBSCENITY

The body of itself is clean, but the caged mind
is a sewer inside, it pollutes, O it pollutes
the guts and the stones and the womb, rots them down,
                                    leaves a rind
of maquillage and pose and malice to shame the brutes.

TOUCH

Since we have become so cerebral
we can't bear to touch or be touched.

Since we are so cerebral
we are humanly out of touch.

And so we must remain.
For if, cerebrally, we force ourselves into touch, into
                                                   contact
physical and fleshly,
we violate ourselves,
we become vicious.

BABY TORTOISE

You know what it is to be born alone,
Baby tortoise!

The first day to heave your feet little by little from
                                        the shell,
Not yet awake,
And remain lapsed on earth,
Not quite alive.

A tiny, fragile, half-animate bean.

To open your tiny beak-mouth, that looks as if it
                                        would never open
Like some iron door;
To lift the upper hawk-beak from the lower base
And reach your skinny neck
And take your first bite at some dim bit of herbage,
Alone, small insect,
Tiny bright-eye,
Slow one.

To take your first solitary bite
And move on your slow, solitary hunt.
Your bright, dark little eye,
Your eye of a dark disturbed night,
Under its slow lid, tiny baby tortoise,
So indomitable.

No one ever heard you complain.

You draw your head forward, slowly, from your little
                                        wimple
And set forward, slow-dragging, on your four-pinned
                                        toes,
Rowing slowly forward.
Wither away, small bird?
Rather like a baby working its limbs,
Except that you make slow, ageless progress
And a baby makes none.

The touch of sun excites you,
And the long ages, and the lingering chill
Make you pause to yawn,
Opening your impervious mouth,
Suddenly beak-shaped, and very wide, like some
                              suddenly gaping pincers;
Soft red tongue, and hard thin gums,
Then close the wedge of your little mountain front,
Your face, baby tortoise.

Do you wonder at the world, as slowly you turn your
                              head in its wimple
And look with laconic, black eyes?
Or is sleep coming over you again,
The non-life?

You are so hard to wake.

Are you able to wonder?
Or is it just your indomitable will and pride of the
                              first life

Looking round
And slowly pitching itself against the inertia
Which had seemed invincible?

The vast inanimate,
And the fine brilliance of your so tiny eye,
Challenger.

Nay, tiny shell-bird.
What a huge vast inanimate it is, that you must row
                                   against,
What an incalculable inertia.

Challenger,
Little Ulysses, fore-runner,
No bigger than my thumb-nail,
Buon viaggio.

All animate creation on your shoulder,
Set forth, little Titan, under your battle-shield.
The ponderous, preponderate,
Inanimate universe;
And you are slowly moving, pioneer, you alone.

How vivid your travelling seems now, in the troubled
                                   sunshine,
Stoic, Ulyssean atom;
Suddenly hasty, reckless, on high toes.

Voiceless little bird,
Resting your head half out of your wimple
In the slow dignity of your eternal pause.
Alone, with no sense of being alone,

And hence six times more solitary;
Fulfilled of the slow passion of pitching through
                              immemorial ages
Your little round house in the midst of chaos.

Over the garden earth,
Small bird,
Over the edge of all things.

Traveller,
With your tail tucked a little on one side
Like a gentleman in a long-skirted coat.

All life carried on your shoulder,
Invincible fore-runner.

TORTOISE SHOUT

I thought he was dumb,
I said he was dumb,
Yet I've heard him cry.

First faint scream,
Out of life's unfathomable dawn,
Far off, so far, like a madness, under the horizon's
                                        dawning rim,
Far, far off, far scream.

Tortoise in extremis.

Why were we crucified into sex?
Why were we not left rounded off, and finished in
                                        ourselves,
As we began,
As he certainly began, so perfectly alone?

A far, was-it-audible scream,
Or did it sound on the plasm direct?

Worse than the cry of the new-born,
A scream,
A yell,
A shout,
A pæan,
A death-agony,
A birth-cry,

A submission,
All tiny, tiny, far away, reptile under the first
                                 dawn.

War-cry, triumph, acute-delight, death-scream
                                reptilian,
Why was the veil torn?
The silken shriek of the soul's torn membrane?
The male soul's membrane
Torn with a shriek half music, half horror.

Crucifixion.
Male tortoise, cleaving behind the hovel-wall of that
                              dense female,
Mounted and tense, spread-eagle, out-reaching out of
                              the shell
In tortoise-nakedness,
Long neck, and long vulnerable limbs extruded,
                      spread-eagle over her house-roof,
And the deep, secret, all-penetrating tail curved
                        beneath her walls,
Reaching and gripping tense, more reaching anguish in
                      uttermost tension
Till suddenly, in the spasm of coition, tupping like a
                      jerking leap, and oh!
Opening its clenched face from his outstretched neck
And giving that fragile yell, that scream,
Super-audible,
From his pink, cleft, old-man's mouth,
Giving up the ghost,
Or screaming in Pentecost, receiving the ghost.

His scream, and his moment's subsidence,

The moment of eternal silence,
Yet unreleased, and after the moment, the sudden,
                    startling jerk of coition, and at once
The inexpressible faint yell
And so on, till the last plasm of my body was melted
                    back
To the primeval rudiments of life, and the secret.

So he tups, and screams
Time after time that frail, torn scream
After each jerk, the longish interval,
The tortoise eternity,
Agelong, reptilian persistence,
Heart-throb, slow heart-throb, persistent for the next
                    spasm.

I remember, when I was a boy,
I heard the scream of a frog, which was caught with
          his foot in the mouth of an up-starting snake;
I remember when I first heard bull-frogs break into
                    sound in the spring;
I remember hearing a wild goose out of the throat of
                    night
Cry loudly, beyond the lake of waters;
I remember the first time, out of a bush in the
          darkness, a nightingale's piercing cries and
          gurgles startled the depths of my soul;
I remember the scream of a rabbit as I went through a
                    wood at midnight;
I remember the heifer in her heat, blorting and
          blorting through the hours, persistent and
                    irrepressible;
I remember my first terror hearing the howl of weird,

                              amorous cats;
I remember the scream of a terrified, injured horse,
                     the sheet-lightning
And running away from the sound of a woman in labor,
                  something like an owl whooing,
And listening inwardly to the first bleat of a lamb,
The first wail of an infant,
And my mother singing to herself,
And the first tenor singing of the passionate throat
       of a young collier, who has long since drunk
                          himself to death,
The first elements of foreign speech
On wild dark lips.

And more than all these,
And less than all these,
This last,
Strange, faint coition yell
Of the male tortoise at extremity,
Tiny from under the very edge of the farthest far-off
                     horizon of life.

The cross,
The wheel on which our silence first is broken,
Sex, which breaks up our integrity, our single
               inviolability, our deep silence
Tearing a cry from us.

Sex, which breaks us into voice, sets us calling
          across the deeps, calling, calling for the
                            complement,
Singing, and calling, and singing again, being
               answered, having found.

Torn, to become whole again, after long seeking for
                              what is lost,
The same cry from the tortoise as from Christ, the
                    Osiris-cry of abandonment,
That which is whole, torn asunder,
That which is in part, finding its whole again
                         throughout the universe.

LETTER FROM TOWN:
ON A GREY MORNING IN MARCH

The clouds are pushing in grey reluctance slowly
                    northward to you,
While north of them all, at the farthest ends, stands
                    one bright-bosomed, aglance
With fire as it guards the wild north cloud-coasts,
                    red-fire seas running through
The rocks where ravens flying to windward melt as a
                    well-shot lance.

You should be out by the orchard, where violets
                    secretly darken the earth,
Or there in the woods of the twilight, with northern
                    wind-flowers shaken astir.
Think of me here in the library, trying and trying a
                    song that is worth
Tears and swords to my heart, arrows no armour will
                    turn or deter.

You tell me the lambs have come, they lie like daisies
                    white in the grass
Of the dark-green hills; new calves in shed; peewits
                    turn after the plough –
It is well for you. For me the navvies work in the
                    road where I pass
And I want to smite in anger the barren rock of each
                    waterless brow.

Like the sough of a wind that is caught up high in the
                              mesh of the budding trees,
A sudden car goes sweeping past, and I strain my soul
                                        to hear
The voice of the furtive triumphant engine as it
                              rushes past like a breeze,
To hear on its mocking triumphance unwitting the
                              after-echo of fear.

AFTERNOON IN SCHOOL
THE LAST LESSON

When will the bell ring, and end this weariness?
How long have they tugged the leash, and strained
apart
My pack of unruly hounds: I cannot start
Them again on a quarry of knowledge they hate to
hunt,

I can haul them and urge them no more.
No more can I endure to bear the brunt
Of the books that lie out on the desks: a full three
score
Of several insults of blotted pages and scrawl
Of slovenly work that they have offered me.
I am sick, and tired more than any thrall
Upon the woodstacks working weariedly.

And shall I take
The last dear fuel and heap it on my soul
Till I rouse my will like a fire to consume
Their dross of indifference, and burn the scroll
Of their insults in punishment? – I will not!
I will not waste myself to embers for them,
Not all for them shall the fires of my life be hot,
For myself a heap of ashes of weariness, till sleep
Shall have raked the embers clear: I will keep
Some of my strength for myself, for if I should sell

It all for them, I should hate them –
- I will sit and wait for the bell.

THE WHITE HORSE

The youth walks up to the white horse, to put its
                                    halter on
and the horse looks at him in silence.
They are so silent, they are in another world.

PIANO

Softly, in the dusk, a woman is singing to me;
Taking me back down the vista of years, till I see
A child sitting under the piano, in the boom of the
                                    tingling strings
And pressing the small, poised feet of a mother who
                                    smiles as she sings.

In spite of myself, the insidious mastery of song
Betrays me back, till the heart of me weeps to belong
To the old Sunday evenings at home, with winter
                                    outside
And hymns in the cosy parlour, the tinkling piano our
                                    guide.

So now it is vain for the singer to burst into clamour
With the great black piano appassionato. The glamour
Of childish days is upon me, my manhood is cast
Down in the flood of remembrance, I weep like a child
                                    for the past.

ROSE OF ALL THE WORLD

I am here myself; as though this heave of effort
At starting other life, fulfilled my own;
Rose-leaves that whirl in colour round a core
Of seed-specks kindled lately and softly blown

By all the blood of the rose-bush into being –
Strange, that the urgent will in me, to set
My mouth on hers in kisses, and so softly
To bring together two strange sparks, beget

Another life from our lives, so should send
The innermost fire of my own dim soul out-spinning
And whirling in blossom of flame and being upon me!
That my completion of manhood should be the
                                    beginning

Another life from mine! For so it looks.
The seed is purpose, blossom accident.
The seed is all in all, the blossom lent
To crown the triumph of this new descent.

Is that it, woman? Does it strike you so?
The Great Breath blowing a tiny seed of fire
Fans out your petals for excess of flame,
Till all your being smokes with fine desire?

Or are we kindled, you and I, to be
One rose of wonderment upon the tree
Of perfect life, and is our possible seed

But the residuum of the ecstasy?

How will you have it? – the rose is all in all,
Or the ripe rose-fruits of the luscious fall?
The sharp begetting, or the child begot?
Our consummation matters, or does it not?

To me it seems the seed is just left over
From the red rose-flowers' fiery transience;
Just orts and slarts; berries that smoulder in the
                                        bush
Which burnt just now with marvellous immanence.

Blossom, my darling, blossom, be a rose
Of roses unchidden and purposeless; a rose
For rosiness only, without an ulterior motive;
For me it is more than enough if the flower unclose.

NEW YEAR'S EVE

There are only two things now,
The great black night scooped out
And this fire-glow.

This fire-glow, the core,
And we the two ripe pips
That are held in store.

Listen, the darkness rings
As it circulates round our fire.
Take off your things.

Your shoulders, your bruised throat!
Your breasts, your nakedness!
This fiery coat!

As the darkness flickers and dips,
As the firelight falls and leaps
From your feet to your lips!

from CRAVING FOR SPRING

I wish it were spring in the world.

Let it be spring!
Come, bubbling, surging tide of sap!
Come, rush of creation!
Come, life! surge through this mass of mortification!
Come, sweep away these exquisite, ghastly
                                    first-flowers,
which are rather last-flowers!
Come, thaw down their cool portentousness, dissolve
                                    them:
snowdrops, straight, death-veined exhalations of white
                        and purple crocuses,
flowers of the penumbra, issue of corruption,
nourished in
mortification,
jets of exquisite finality;
Come, spring, make havoc of them!

•

I want the fine, kindling wine-sap of spring,
gold, and of inconceivably fine, quintessential
                                    brightness,
rare almost as beams, yet overwhelmingly potent,
strong like the greatest force of world-balancing.

•

I wish it were spring, thundering
delicate, tender spring.

•

Oh, in the spring, the bluebell bows him down for very
                                          exuberance,
exulting with secret warm excess
bowed down with his inner magnificence!

•

The gush of spring is strong enough
to play with the globe of earth like a ball on a fountain;
At the same time it opens the tiny hands of the hazel
with such infinite patience.
The power of the rising, golden, all-creative sap could
                                    take the earth
and heave it off among the stars, into the invisible;
the same sets the throstle at sunset on a bough
singing against the blackbird;
comes out in the hesitating tremor of the primrose,
and betrays its candour in the round white strawberry
                                       flower,
is dignified in the foxglove, like a Red-Indian brave.

Ah come, come quickly, spring!
Come and lift us towards our culmination, we myriads;
we who have never flowered, like patient cactuses.
Come and lift us to our end, to blossom, bring us to our
                                       summer,
we who are winter-weary in the winter of the world.

from MANIFESTO

But then came another hunger
very deep, and ravening;
the very body's body crying out
with a hunger more frightening, more profound
than stomach or throat or even the mind;
redder than death, more clamorous.

The hunger for the woman.

•

Let them praise desire who will,
but only fulfilment will do,
real fulfilment, nothing short.
It is our ratification,
our heaven, as a matter of fact.
Immortality, the heaven, is only a projection of this
                    strange but actual fulfilment,
here in the flesh.

•

To be, or not to be, is still the question.
This ache for being is the ultimate hunger. I want her
though, to take the same from me.
She touches me as if I were herself, her own.
She has not realised yet, that fearful thing, that I am the
                              other,

she thinks we are all of one piece.
It is painfully untrue.

I want her to touch me at last, ah, on the roof and quick
                              of my darkness
and perish on me, as I have perished on her.

Then, we shall be two and distinct, we shall have each
                              our separate being.
And that will be pure existence, real liberty.
Till then, we are confused, a mixture, unresolved,
                              unextricated one from the other.
It is in pure, unutterable resolvedness, distinction of
                              being, that one is free,
not in mixing, merging, not in similarity.
When she has put her hand on my secret, darkest
                    sources, the darkest outgoings,
when it has struck home to her, like a death, "this is
                              him!"
she has no part in it, no part whatever,
it is the terrible *other*,
when she knows the fearful *other flesh*, ah, darkness
                    unfathomable and fearful, contiguous and
                                        concrete,
when she is slain against me, and lies in a heap like one
                              outside the house,
when she passes away as I have passed away,
being pressed up against the *other*,
then I shall be glad, I shall not be confused with her,
I shall be cleared, distinct, single as if burnished in silver,
having no adherence, no adhesion anywhere,
one clear, burnished, isolated being, unique,
and she also, pure, isolated, complete,

two of us, unutterably distinguished, and in unutterable
                                                 conjunction.

Then we shall be free, freer than angels, ah, perfect.

After than, there will only remain that all men detach
themselves and become unique,
that we are all detached, moving in freedom more than
                                                 the angels,
conditioned only by our own pure single being,
having no laws but the laws of our own being.

Every human being will then by like a flower,
                                        untrammelled.
Every movement will be direct.
Only to be will such delight, we cover our faces when
                                        we think of it
Lest our faces betray us to some untimely fiend.

Every man himself, and therefore, a surpassing
                                 singleness of mankind.
The blazing tiger will spring upon the deer, undimmed,
the hen will nestle over her chickens,
we shall love, we shall hate,
but it will be like music, sheer utterance,
issuing straight out of the unknown,
the lightning and the rainbows appearing in us
unbidden,
unchecked,
like ambassadors.

We shall not look before and after.
We shall *be*, *now*.

We shall know in full.
We, the mystic NOW.

A Note On D.H. Lawrence

David Herbert Lawrence polarizes readers and writers as few other writers do. People either love or hate him. Few are indifferent. In the opinion of many he is the key writer in English of the 20th century. Many writers have been influenced by Lawrence: Nin, Miller, Durrell, Mailer, Drabble, Carver, Aldington, Orwell, Hughes, Auden, Bukowski, Burgess, Creeley, Williams, etc. Many people championed Lawrence: Leavis, Bragg, Murray, Sagar, Aldington, Nin, Miller, Moore. Henry Miller typifies those who love Lawrence: he is a Christ, a hero, a passionate soul, a heroic genius, a visionary, etc. This view – of Lawrence as a heroic genius of love and life – is still held by many today.

For Anais Nin Lawrence was a brilliant poet of sensuality. She loves him because he wrote about the experience of being a woman; and because he reclaimed women's sexual experiences from obscurity.[1] For Nin, Lawrence was the re-inventor of poetic realism, and his subject matter was also Nin's – emotional transformation. Of *Lady Chatterley's Lover* Nin writes, in her usual intuitive way:

> A vigorous and impetuous style carries the weight of intense physical and imaginative emotions and in the end unites them in a brilliant

---

[1] Nin, *The Journals of Anais Nin*, ed. Gunther Stuhlmann, 6 vols, Quartet 1974/6/9 3, 210-1

fusion of physical-mysticism.[2]

For Aldington 'both in living and in writing Lawrence was a genius, but...'.[3] All the criticism of Lawrence discusses his life as well as his art. His life is fused with his art. Critics have found it impossible to untie the art from the life (even though Lawrence states 'Trust the tale'). The main critics have all found it necessary to talk about the man as well as the artist: Clarke, Leavis, Moore, Kinkead-Weekes, Spilka, Hough, Draper, Daleski, Kermode, Sagar, Holbrook, Moynahan, Pinion, Salgado, Worthen, etc. Lawrence the man has fascinated critics and readers as few other artists have (one thinks of Van Gogh, Rimbaud, Byron, Emily Bronte).

Most criticism of Lawrence does not fail to mention some event or characteristic of his life. Feminists will point out that he was a wife-beater, to support their argument that he was a misogynist. Other critics will point to his relationship with Murray as the basis of his homosexual discourses. Even more tiresomely, some critics will note that this or that real-life person was the basis of this or that character (Frieda and Louie Burrows for Ursula, Bertrand Russell for Sir Joshua Matteson, etc).[4]

The people who love Lawrence really love him. Leavis called him 'incomparably the greatest creative writer in English of our time...one of the greatest English writers of any time'.[5] For Mailer, Lawrence was 'a man more beautiful than we can guess'.[6] For Holbrook Lawrence gets it wrong and *Lady Chatterley's Lover*, exalted by Nin as Lawrence's best book, is

---

[2] *D.H. Lawrence: An Unprofessional Study*, Black Spring 1985, 108

[3] Richard Aldington: *Portrait of a Genius, But...*, Reader's Union/Heinemann 1951, ,vi

[4] see, for example: Keith Brown, ed.: *Rethinking Lawrence*, Open University Press, Milton Keynes 1990; Anthony Burgess: *Flame Into Being: The Life and Work of D.H. Lawrence*, Heinemann 1985; H. Coombes, ed: *D.H. Lawrence: A Critical Anthology*, Penguin 1973; Carol Dix: *D.H. Lawrence and Women*, Macmillan 1990; Christopher Heywood, ed: *D.H. Lawrence: New Studies*, Macmillan 1987; David Holbrook: *The Quest for Love*, Methuen 1964; F.R.Leavis: *D.H. Lawrence: Novelist*, Penguin 1964; Jeffrey Meyers, ed: *The Legacy of D.H. Lawrence: New Essays*, Macmillan 1987; Harry T.Moore: *The Intelligent Heart: The Story of D.H. Lawrence*, Penguin 1960; *The Priest of Love: A Life of D.H. Lawrence*, Penguin 1976; Moore and Warren Roberts: *D.H. Lawrence*, Thames and Hudson 1966/88; F.B.Pinion: *A D.H. Lawrence Companion: Life, Thought and Works*, Macmillan 1978; Keith Sagar: *A D.H. Lawrence Handbook*, Manchester University Press 1982

[5] *D.H. Lawrence*, op.cit., 18

[6] Norman Mailer: *The Prisoner of Sex*, New American Library/Signet 1971, 110

'cranky and false' (*A Quest for Love*, 322).

Each generation invents Lawrence anew. In the 60s Lawrence became a Hippy, a Beatnik, a liberated Bohemian who advocated 'free love' and back-to-Nature eco-friendly politics. In the Seventies feminists attacked Lawrence and explored his ideological ambiguities. In the 80s Lawrence has proved to be as popular as ever - there was a flurry of critical activity during the 1985 centenary celebrations. Lawrence's politics and polemics continue to antagonize people, but his fiction remains at the core of his achievement and critical status.

Lawrence's poetry, however, is, generally, far less successful than his fiction. It is often loose, rather than fluid, unstructured rather than 'free', messy rather than well-defined. It is a poetry, as Lawrence stresses, of the moment, a poetry in the process of becoming, constantly dissolving. In the Foreword to his *Pansies*, he wrote of that breathless transience, embodied for him in the life of a flower: the breath of the moment, and one eternal moment easily contradicting the next eternal moment. Only don't nail the pansy down. You won't keep it any better if you do.'[7] In the Introduction to the American edition of *New Poems*, Lawrence writes:

> Let me feel the mud and the heavens in my lotus. Let me feel the heavy, silting, sucking mud, the spinning of sky winds. Let me feel them both in purest contact, the nakedness of sucking weight, nakedly passing radiance. Give me nothing fixed, set, static. Don't give me the infinite or the eternal: nothing of infinity, nothing of eternity. Give me the still, white seething, the incandescence and the coldness of the incarnate moment: the moment, the quick of all change and haste and opposition: the moment, the immediate present, the Now. The immediate moment is not a drop of water running downstream. It is the source and issue, the bubbling up of the stream. Here, in this very instant moment, up bubbles the stream of time, out of the wells of futurity, flowing on to the oceans of the past. The source, the issue, the creative quick. There is poetry of this immediate present, instant poetry, as well as poetry of the infinite past and the infinite future. The seething poetry of the incarnate Now is supreme, beyond even the everlasting of the before and after.[8]

Lawrence's typical poetry occurs in poems such as 'Sicilian Cyclamens', 'Snake' and 'Snap-Dragon', longish, loose poems with a lot of space that allows Lawrence to explore his subject. The problems arise when Lawrence loses his hold on the poetics and the result is a series of effects or lines. Much of Lawrence's poetry, his worst poetry, occurs in

---

[7] Lawrence in March 1929, quoted in *The Complete Poems*, 424

[8] Lawrence, in *Complete Poems*, 182-3

those short lyrics that aim to preach, such as 'For all That', 'Moth and Rust', Doors', 'The Breath of life', 'The Property Question', 'Welcome Death', Dies Irae' and 'Stop It'.

The preaching, polemical poems are Lawrence at his worst as a poet. They are ideas-poems, poems of thoughts, epigrams or maxims. Yet they do not have the compression or lucidity of, for instance, the Greek anthology epigrams, or those of Novalis. The short lyric 'Immortality' is typical:

The real immortality, as far as I can see it
Lies in forcing yourself or somebody else
Against all your deeper instincts and your intuition.[9]

Lawrence's polemical poems are like the polemical passages in his novels, those passages where Lawrence the Preacher and Politician gets on his soapbox. In the novels, these are the worst moments (think of *The Plumed Serpent* or *The Lost Girl*). I have included some of the preachy poems here ('Touch Comes' and 'Future Religion', among others), as they are a part of Lawrence's poetic output. He's always telling the reader what to do ('[s]o the only thing to do, is to keep still, to hold still at any price,/ To learn to contain ourselves' he pronounces in 'What's To Be Done?').[10] Much as his characters are always telling each other what to do.

The poems about beasts are some of Lawrence's more successful pieces ('Snake', 'She-Goat', ''The Ass', 'Kangaroo', Mountain Lion'). The 'Tortoise' poems are Lawrence's most wrathful, with their condemnation of deathly sex: '

His scream, and his moment's subsidence,
The moment of eternal silence,
Yet unreleased, and after the moment, the sudden, startling jerk of
                                        coition, and at once
the inexpressible faint yell -
And so on, till the last plasm of my body was melted back
To the primeval rudiments of life, and the secret.

So he tups, and screams
Time after time that frail, torn scream
After each jerk, the longish interval,
The tortoise eternity,

9 in *Complete Poems*, 837
10 in *The Complete Poems*, 839

Age-long, reptilian persistence,
Heart-throb, slow heart-throb, persistent for the next spasm.[11]

And in another animal poem he writes of '[o]rgasm after orgasm after orgasm' (in 'He-Goat'.)[12]

The ruthless depiction of sex and death in Lawrence's poetry is familiar to anyone who has read *Women in Love*, where characters go black with rage and lust. This (sensational) side of Lawrence is well-documented, and much discussed. But just as typical is the poet who writes lengthily and lyrically of flowers and suns ('Hibiscus and Salvia Flowers', 'Purple Anemones', 'Almond Blossom'), or bucolic Greek romances ('Hymn to Priapus', or social commentary ('Nottingham's New University'), or of fruit 'Pomegranate', 'Figs', 'Grapes'). Lawrence wrote admiringly of Cézanne, claiming that the painter presented the viewer with the essence of an apple, the 'appleness' of the fruit. Similarly, the poet Rainer Maria Rilke carefully sketched the is-ness of objects in many poems (such as the famous 'Archaic Torso of Apollo', 'The Panther', 'The gazelle', 'The Bowl of Roses' and 'Blue Hydrangea'). Rilke's notion of 'Kunst-Ding, the 'thingness' or *innigkeit* of an object has much in common with Lawrence's still life poems.

Lawrence actually covers a surprisingly wide range of subjects, far wider than, say, Robert Graves or Thomas Hardy or John Keats. Among other poets, there is no one quite like him. Like every poet, he has his pet notions, and keeps hacking away at them (the river of blood of the *Sons and Lovers* era, the 'democracy of touch' from *Lady Chatterley's Lover*, the Christological *machismo* of *The Plumed Serpent* lyrics, hatred of labour, love of all things Mediterranean, the primacy of the body - 'the very body's body crying out' he writes in 'Manifesto',[13] etc).

Lawrence is still widely discussed because, perhaps, his art is challenging, on a number of levels. Writers such as Miller, Nin, Bragg, Carver, Williams and Durrell invoke his name because he is the epitome of passion. He is the creative artist who never stopped creating, who worked heroically, like Van Gogh or Turner, non-stop, right to the end. He was full of conviction,. His views kept changing, but he believed in them passionately. He was an honest artist, an intuitive seer, the working-class boy from the sticks who made good, who aimed as high as possible, who came closer than most to achieving his goal.

---

[11] in *The Complete Poems*, 365

[12] *The Complete Poems*, 382

[13] in *The Complete Poems*, 264

Critically, Lawrence is a celebrated modernist, championed by such champion critics as F.R. Leavis. But Lawrence can be approached in all sorts of ways critically, as the many books on him show. Like Joyce and Woolf, he is one of the key modernists. He draws together discussions on politics, religion, philosophy, sexuality, language and a host of other topics. His popularity as a subject of criticism must be due to this multivalence - the way Lawrence engages so many aspects of contemporary culture.

Lawrence does have many strange ideas - ideas that seem strange at first, but have been a part of the philosophical underbelly of Western culture (found in Gnosticism, the troubadours and courtly love, numerology, bestiaries, symbolism, etc).

Lawrence's notions - his peculiar sense of physiology, for instance (embodied for me in words such as *loins*) - are not so much strange as strangely (and passionately) expressed. It is the sheer force and energy of Lawrence's communication that makes him fascinating. While other artists might um and er about sexuality, Lawrence dives right in, and says what he thinks, in a powerful manner.

Then there is his poetry, which can be remarkably lucid. His phrasing is not awkward, as Hardy's sometimes was. He is not obscure. His main aesthetic tactic is musical repetition (which also makes him sometimes tiresome to read). He uses simple mechanisms of poetry - comparisons, colourful adjectives, vivid verbs and metaphors, although his stanzas often make unusual shapes and patterns. His innovation was to somehow describe subtle, inner states of being by using simple, everyday words (such as *darkness, touch, strange*). 'Darkness' is an ordinary word, describing something that covers half the planet every night. Yet in Lawrence's hands it becomes a powerful way of describing a state of being. If you write 'she walked home through the darkness' you have a simple statement. But if you write 'the darkness was inside her as she walked' you have a psychological insight; action has become emotion. This is Lawrence's realm, where naturalism becomes symbolism, realism becomes emotionalism and politics becomes psychology.

His life and personality adds charisma and weight to his art, as with Van Gogh, Rimbaud and Byron. But his colourful personas do not cheapen his art, nor take away from the fact that he was a marvellous writer, if not always a successful poet. But poems such as 'Tropic', 'Swan', 'Manifesto' and 'Whales Weep Not!' are pure Lawrence, purely his own creation, his own poetic realm. And poems such as 'Bavarian Gentians' are rightly celebrated. It is poems such as these which become not merely adjuncts to the fiction.

J.R.R. Tolkien
The Books, The Films, The Whole Cultural Phenomenon

by Jeremy Mark Robinson

A new critical study of J.R.R. Tolkien, creator of Middle-earth and author of *The Lord of the Rings, The Hobbit* and *The Silmarillion*, among other books.

This new critical study explores Tolkien's major writings (*The Lord of the Rings, The Hobbit, Beowulf: The Monster and the Critics, The Letters, The Silmarillion* and *The History of Middle-earth* volumes); Tolkien and fairy tales; the mythological, political and religious aspects of Tolkien's Middle-earth; the critics' response to Tolkien's fiction over the decades; the Tolkien industry (merchandizing, toys, role-playing games, posters, Tolkien societies, conferences and the like); Tolkien in visual and fantasy art; the cultural aspects of The Lord of the Rings (from the 1950s to the present); Tolkien's fiction's relationship with other fantasy fiction, such as C.S. Lewis and *Harry Potter*; and the TV, radio and film versions of Tolkien's books, including the 2001-03 Hollywood interpretations of *The Lord of the Rings*.

This new book draws on contemporary cultural theory and analysis and offers a sympathetic and illuminating (and sceptical) account of the Tolkien phenomenon. This book is designed to appeal to the general reader (and viewer) of Tolkien: it is written in a clear, jargon-free and easily-accessible style.

754pp   ISBN 1-86171-057-7   £25.00 / $37.50

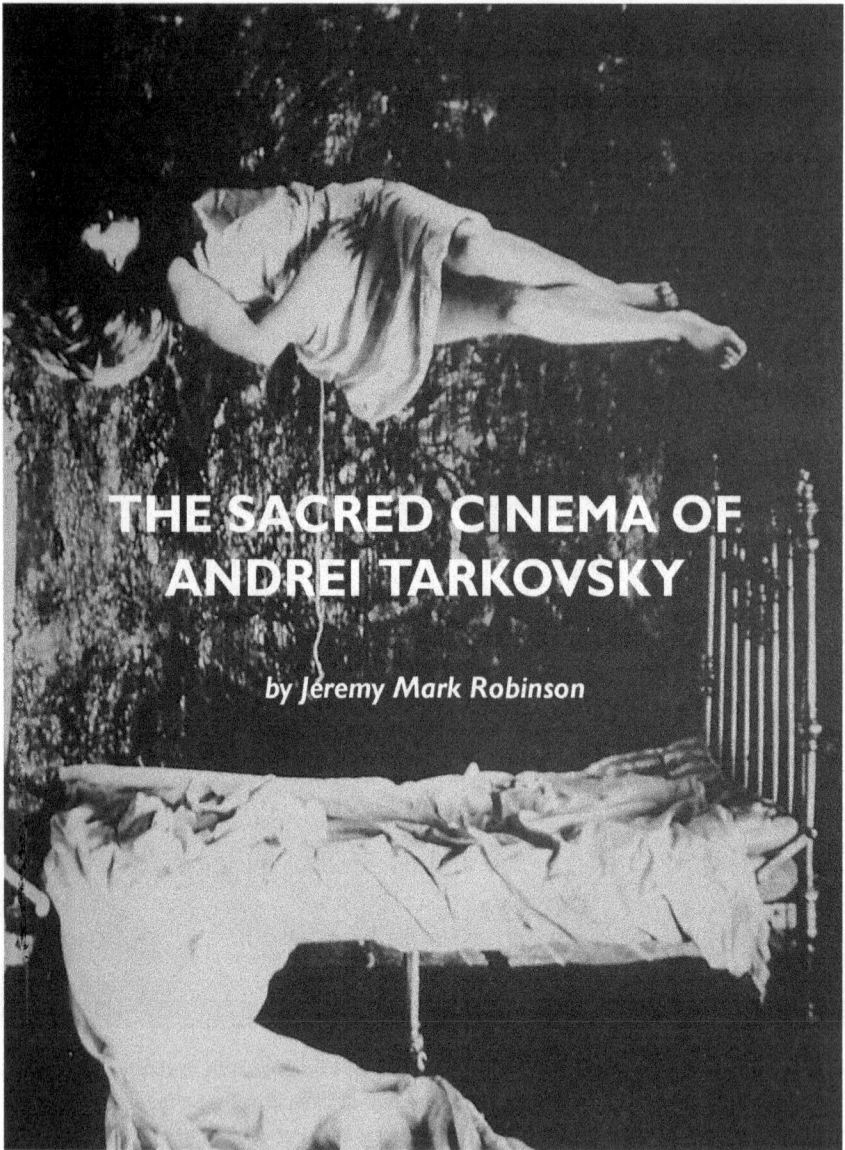

THE SACRED CINEMA OF ANDREI TARKOVSKY

by Jeremy Mark Robinson

A new study of the Russian filmmaker Andrei Tarkovsky (1932-1986), director of seven feature films, including *Andrei Roublyov, Mirror, Solaris, Stalker* and *The Sacrifice*.
This is one of the most comprehensive and detailed studies of Tarkovsky's cinema available. Every film is explored in depth, with scene-by-scene analyses. All aspects of Tarkovsky's output are critiqued, including editing, camera, staging, script, budget, collaborations, production, sound, music, performance and spirituality. Tarkovsky is placed with a European New Wave tradition of filmmaking, alongside directors like Ingmar Bergman, Carl Theodor Dreyer, Pier Paolo Pasolini and Robert Bresson.
An essential addition to film studies.

Illustrations: 150 b/w, 4 colour. 682 pages. First edition. Hardback.

Publisher: Crescent Moon Publishing. Distributor: Gardners Books.

ISBN 1-86171-096-8 (9781861710963) £60.00 / $105.00

The Best of Peter Redgrove's Poetry
The Book of Wonders

by Peter Redgrove, edited and introduced by Jeremy Robinson

Poems of wet shirts and 'wonder-awakening dresses'; honey, wasps and bees; orchards and apples; rivers, seas and tides; storms, rain, weather and clouds; waterworks; labyrinths; amazing perfumes; the Cornish landscape (Penzance, Perranporth, Falmouth, Boscastle, the Lizard and Scilly Isles); the sixth sense and 'extra-sensuous perception'; witchcraft; alchemical vessels and laboratories; yoga; menstruation; mines, minerals and stones; sand dunes; mud-baths; mythology; dreaming; vulvas; and lots of sex magic. This book gathers together poetry (and prose) from every stage of Redgrove's career, and every book. It includes pieces that have only appeared in small presses and magazines, and in uncollected form.

'Peter Redgrove is really an extraordinary poet' (George Szirtes, *Quarto* magazine)
'Peter Redgrove is one of the few significant poets now writing... His 'means' are indeed bril-liant and delightful. Technically he is a poet essentially of brilliant and unexpected images...he never disappoints' (Kathleen Raine, *Temenos* magazine).

240pp   ISBN 1-86171-063-1   2nd edition   £19.99 / $29.50

Sex–Magic–Poetry–Cornwall
A Flood of Poems

by Peter Redgrove. Edited with an essay by Jeremy Robinson

A marvellous collection of poems by one of Britain's best but underrated poets, Peter Redgrove. This book brings together some of Redgrove's wildest and most passionate works, creating a 'flood' of poetry. Philip Hobsbaum called Redgrove 'the great poet of our time', while Angela Carter said: 'Redgrove's language can light up a page.' Redgrove ranks alongside Ted Hughes and Sylvia Plath. He is in every way a 'major poet'. Robinson's essay analyzes all of Redgrove's poetic work, including his use of sex magic, natural science, menstruation, psy-chology, myth, alchemy and feminism.
A new edition, including a new introduction, new preface and new bibliography.

'Robinson's enthusiasm is winning, and his perceptive readings are supported by a very useful bibliography' (*Acumen* magazine)
'*Sex-Magic-Poetry-Cornwall* is a very rich essay... It is like a brightly-lighted box. (Peter Redgrove)
'This is an excellent selection of poetry and an extensive essay on the themes and theories of this unusual poet by Jeremy Robinson' (*Chapman* magazine)

220pp   New, 3rd edition   ISBN 1-86171-070-4   £14.99 / $23.50

THE ART OF
ANDY GOLDSWORTHY

COMPLETE WORKS: SPECIAL EDITION
(PAPERBACK and HARDBACK)

by William Malpas

A new, special edition of the study of the contemporary British sculptor, Andy Goldsworthy, including a new introduction, new bibliography and many new illustrations.

This is the most comprehensive, up-to-date, well-researched and in-depth account of Goldsworthy's art available anywhere.

Andy Goldsworthy makes land art. His sculpture is a sensitive, intuitive response to nature, light, time, growth, the seasons and the earth. Goldsworthy's environmental art is becoming ever more popular: 1993's art book *Stone* was a bestseller; the press raved about Goldsworthy taking over a number of London West End art galleries in 1994; during 1995 Goldsworthy designed a set of Royal Mail stamps and had a show at the British Museum. Malpas surveys all of Goldsworthy's art, and analyzes his relation with other land artists such as Robert Smithson, Walter de Maria, Richard Long and David Nash, and his place in the contemporary British art scene.

The Art of Andy Goldsworthy discusses all of Goldsworthy's important and recent exhibitions and books, including the *Sheepfolds* project; the TV documentaries; *Wood* (1996); the New York Holocaust memorial (2003); and Goldsworthy's collaboration on a dance performance.

Illustrations: 70 b/w, 1 colour. 330 pages. New, special, 2nd edition.
Publisher: Crescent Moon Publishing. Distributor: Gardners Books.

ISBN 1-86171-059-3 (9781861710598) (Paperback) £25.00 / $44.00

ISBN 1-86171-080-1 (9781861710802) (Hardback) £60.00 / $105.00

CRESCENT MOON PUBLISHING

ARTS, PAINTING, SCULPTURE

The Art of Andy Goldsworthy: Complete Works(Pbk)
The Art of Andy Goldsworthy: Complete Works (Hbk)
Andy Goldsworthy in Close-Up (Pbk)
Andy Goldsworthy in Close-Up (Hbk)
Land Art: A Complete Guide
Richard Long: The Art of Walking
The Art of Richard Long: Complete Works (Pbk)
The Art of Richard Long: Complete Works (Hbk)
Richard Long in Close-Up
Land Art In the UK
Land Art in Close-Up
Installation Art in Close-Up
Minimal Art and Artists In the 1960s and After
Colourfield Painting
Land Art DVD, TV documentary
Andy Goldsworthy DVD, TV documentary
The Erotic Object: Sexuality in Sculpture From Prehistory to the Present Day
Sex in Art: Pornography and Pleasure in Painting and Sculpture
Postwar Art
Sacred Gardens: The Garden in Myth, Religion and Art
Glorification: Religious Abstraction in Renaissance and 20th Century Art
Early Netherlandish Painting
Leonardo da Vinci
Piero della Francesca
Giovanni Bellini
Fra Angelico: Art and Religion in the Renaissance
Mark Rothko: The Art of Transcendence
Frank Stella: American Abstract Artist
Jasper Johns: Painting By Numbers
Brice Marden
Alison Wilding: The Embrace of Sculpture
Vincent van Gogh: Visionary Landscapes
Eric Gill: Nuptials of God
Constantin Brancusi: Sculpting the Essence of Things
Max Beckmann
Egon Schiele: Sex and Death In Purple Stockings
Delizioso Fotografico Fervore: Works In Process 1
Sacro Cuore: Works In Process 2
The Light Eternal: J.M.W. Turner
The Madonna Glorified: Karen Arthurs

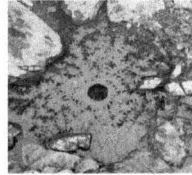

LITERATURE

J.R.R. Tolkien: The Books, The Films, The Whole Cultural Phenomenon
Harry Potter
Sexing Hardy: Thomas Hardy and Feminism
Thomas Hardy's *Tess of the d'Urbervilles*
Thomas Hardy's *Jude the Obscure*
Thomas Hardy: The Tragic Novels
Love and Tragedy: Thomas Hardy
The Poetry of Landscape in Hardy
Wessex Revisited: Thomas Hardy and John Cowper Powys
Wolfgang Iser: Essays
Petrarch, Dante and the Troubadours
Maurice Sendak and the Art of Children's Book Illustration
Andrea Dworkin
Cixous, Irigaray, Kristeva: The *Jouissance* of French Feminism
Julia Kristeva: Art, Love, Melancholy, Philosophy, Semiotics and Psychoanalysis
Hélene Cixous I Love You: The *Jouissance* of Writing
Luce Irigaray: Lips, Kissing, and the Politics of Sexual Difference
Peter Redgrove: Here Comes the Flood
Peter Redgrove: Sex-Magic-Poetry-Cornwall
Lawrence Durrell: Between Love and Death, East and West
Love, Culture & Poetry: Lawrence Durrell
Cavafy: Anatomy of a Soul
German Romantic Poetry: Goethe, Novalis, Heine, Hölderlin, Schlegel, Schiller
Feminism and Shakespeare
Shakespeare: Selected Sonnets
Shakespeare: Love, Poetry & Magic
The Passion of D.H. Lawrence
D.H. Lawrence: Symbolic Landscapes
D.H. Lawrence: Infinite Sensual Violence
Rimbaud: Arthur Rimbaud and the Magic of Poetry
The Ecstasies of John Cowper Powys
Sensualism and Mythology: The Wessex Novels of John Cowper Powys
Amorous Life: John Cowper Powys and the Manifestation of Affectivity (H.W. Fawkner)
Postmodern Powys: New Essays on John Cowper Powys (Joe Boulter)
Rethinking Powys: Critical Essays on John Cowper Powys
Paul Bowles & Bernardo Bertolucci
Rainer Maria Rilke
In the Dim Void: Samuel Beckett
Samuel Beckett Goes into the Silence
André Gide: Fiction and Fervour
Jackie Collins and the Blockbuster Novel
Blinded By Her Light: The Love-Poetry of Robert Graves
The Passion of Colours: Travels In Mediterranean Lands
Poetic Forms
The Dolphin-Boy

POETRY

The Best of Peter Redgrove's Poetry
Peter Redgrove: Here Comes The Flood
Peter Redgrove: Sex-Magic-Poetry-Cornwall
Ursula Le Guin: Walking In Cornwall
Dante: Selections From the Vita Nuova
Petrarch, Dante and the Troubadours
William Shakespeare: Selected Sonnets
Blinded By Her Light: The Love-Poetry of Robert Graves
Emily Dickinson: Selected Poems
Emily Brontë: Poems
Thomas Hardy: Selected Poems
Percy Bysshe Shelley: Poems
John Keats: Selected Poems
D.H. Lawrence: Selected Poems
Edmund Spenser: Poems
John Donne: Poems
Henry Vaughan: Poems
Sir Thomas Wyatt: Poems
Robert Herrick: Selected Poems
Rilke: Space, Essence and Angels in the Poetry of Rainer Maria Rilke
Rainer Maria Rilke: Selected Poems
Friedrich Hölderlin: Selected Poems
Arseny Tarkovsky: Selected Poems
Arthur Rimbaud: Selected Poems
Arthur Rimbaud: A Season in Hell
Arthur Rimbaud and the Magic of Poetry
D.J. Enright: By-Blows
Jeremy Reed: Brigitte's Blue Heart
Jeremy Reed: Claudia Schiffer's Red Shoes
Gorgeous Little Orpheus
Radiance: New Poems
Crescent Moon Book of Nature Poetry
Crescent Moon Book of Love Poetry
Crescent Moon Book of Mystical Poetry
Crescent Moon Book of Elizabethan Love Poetry
Crescent Moon Book of Metaphysical Poetry
Crescent Moon Book of Romantic Poetry
Pagan America: New American Poetry

MEDIA, CINEMA, FEMINISM and CULTURAL STUDIES

J.R.R. Tolkien: The Books, The Films, The Whole Cultural Phenomenon
Harry Potter
Cixous, Irigaray, Kristeva: The *Jouissance* of French Feminism
Julia Kristeva: Art, Love, Melancholy, Philosophy, Semiotics and   Psychoanalysis
Luce Irigaray: Lips, Kissing, and the Politics of Sexual Difference
Hélene Cixous I Love You: The *Jouissance* of Writing
Andrea Dworkin
'Cosmo Woman': The World of Women's Magazines
Women in Pop Music
Discovering the Goddess (Geoffrey Ashe)
The Poetry of Cinema
The Sacred Cinema of Andrei Tarkovsky (Pbk and Hbk)
Paul Bowles & Bernardo Bertolucci
Media Hell: Radio, TV and the Press
An Open Letter to the BBC
Detonation Britain: Nuclear War in the UK
Feminism and Shakespeare
Wild Zones: Pornography, Art and Feminism
Sex in Art: Pornography and Pleasure in Painting and Sculpture
Sexing Hardy: Thomas Hardy and Feminism

In my view *The Light Eternal* is among the very best of all the material I read on Turner. (Douglas Graham, director of the Turner Museum, Denver, Colorado)

The Light Eternal is a model monograph, an exemplary job. The subject matter of the book is beautifully organised and dead on beam. (Lawrence Durrell)

It is amazing for me to see my work treated with such passion and respect. (Andrea Dworkin)

Sex-Magic-Poetry-Cornwall is a very rich essay... It is like a brightly-lighted box. (Peter Redgrove)

CRESCENT MOON PUBLISHING
P.O. Box 393, Maidstone, Kent, ME14 5XU, United Kingdom.
01622-729593 (UK) 01144-1622-729593 (US) 0044-1622-729593 (other territories)
cresmopub@yahoo.co.uk   www.crescentmoon.org.uk

www.ingramcontent.com/pod-product-compliance
Lightning Source LLC
Chambersburg PA
CBHW062013040426
42447CB00010B/2010